The Catholic Church in Mission

Highlights of church teaching since 1891

EUGENE DANIELS

MARC

A division of World Vision International
121 East Huntington Drive
Monrovia, California 91016-3400 USA

The Catholic Church in Mission

Highlights of church teaching since 1891

by Eugene Daniels

ISBN: 0-912552-80-8

Published by MARC, a division of World Vision International, 121 East Huntington Drive, Monrovia, California 91016-3400, U.S.A.

Printed in the United States of America. Front and back covers designed by Edler Graphics, Monrovia, California.

Contents

Preface

THE ORGANIZATION with which I serve, World Vision, is an international partnership of Christians working together with the poor in their process of transformation. Holistic development programs that promote human and social transformation provide an avenue for creative partnership with people in community. Holism suggests equal concern for activities that move people towards sustainable development and the formation of mature Christian faith. Together, they point towards the fullness of kingdom life.

Throughout what may be termed the "world of the poor," the Roman Catholic Church, through its various organs, is involved in programs that parallel World Vision's ministry. Historically, though, cooperation between these two expressions of the body of Christ has been severely restricted.

In the course of its organizational development, however, World Vision has become a Christian agency with broad ecumenical interests. It draws spiritual and material resources from all the historic Christian communions and is committed to active participation in the holistic mission of the universal church.

This booklet was undertaken to provide resource material for a process of reflecting on the meaning and implications of inclusiveness in church relationships, particularly as it relates to the Roman Catholic Church.

My study traces the emergence of development and evangelization as distinct strands in the broader context of Catholic social teaching. This will contribute to our understanding of how theological and ecclesiological diversity can be accommodated, and how broader cooperation will contribute to the holistic mission of the church.

Eugene Daniels
April 1993

Introduction

AMONG EVANGELICALS there is a growing consensus that evangelism and development are integrated and essential aspects of human transformation. Consequently, holistic development programs have become standard expressions of Christian mission.

Holism suggests equal concern for moving people (and communities) towards sustainable development and the formation of mature Christian faith. This approach voids the old debate of which is more important: evangelism or development. It assumes the biblical model of bringing people into the fullness of life to which Jesus directed his earthly ministry (John 10:10).

Sadly, though, both evangelicals and Roman Catholics overlook the convergence of these two strands of mission in the Roman Catholic tradition. As a result, relatively little has been accomplished in moving towards the common witness envisioned by Vatican Council II and the Evangelical-Roman Catholic Dialogue on Mission (see UR: 12 and ERCDOM 1986: 84-86).

This study is an attempt to provide resource material that will encourage reflection on some commonalities shared by evangelicals and Roman Catholics. It traces the emergences of development and evangelization as distinct threads in the broad fabric of Catholic social teaching.

The literature which documents Catholic social teaching is vast. This survey concentrates on official documents that are generally accepted as being pivotal statements on the church's understanding of mission.

Roman Catholic teaching authority is found in papal pronouncements, conciliar decrees, and conference reports approved by the Vatican. For non-Catholics, these documents may appear to contain a certain amount of ambiguity. Robert McAfee Brown has aptly commented on the difficulty Protestants encounter in seeking to understand "episcopal prose." He notes that official documents tend to be "rambling, repetitious and occasionally contradictory" (Eagleson and Sharper: 330).

Pronouncements seem to contain endless references to previous statements and documents, needing a careful grounding of papal thought in established precedents. However, this should not obscure the profound evolution within the Catholic understanding of mission.

Pre-Vatican II

CATHOLIC SCHOLARS AGREE that modern social teaching begins with Pope Leo XIII's encyclical, *The Condition of Labor* (*Rerum Novarum* - RN), written in 1891. The pope was troubled because the Industrial Revolution concentrated wealth in the hands of a small group and excluded poor workers from its enjoyment. He saw that this contradicted the will of God who gave the earth to all humanity to use and dispose of. He called the church to speak out on behalf of workers because he understood that social issues affect both religion and morality

"Leo XIII was convinced that the church, at the same time that she has the specific mission of *proclaiming the Gospel*, has the duty of insisting on the social consequences deriving from it. His great concern was that we could witness the beginning of a kind of alienation process separating the Gospel from industrial society and, as a consequence, causing the Gospel to lose all its influence in solving social problems" (John Paul II in "Social and Political Problems": 7). *Rerum Novarum* is important because it brought the force of church authority to bear on the problem of the wealthy exploiting workers and on the need for moral reform.

Forty years later Pope Pius XI issued *Reconstruction of the Social Order* (*Quadragesimo Anno* - QA). He moved the church beyond *Rerum Novarum* by pointing out that the powerful used society's structures as a means to oppress the poor. Pius called for a new social and economic order in which governments should initiate reforms to improve conditions among the exploited masses. He recognized that for change to take place, economic institutions required a "spirit of justice" (QA: 88).

The emergence of a new paradigm

In 1960, on the seventieth anniversary of *Rerum Novarum*, Pope John XXIII issued the well-known *On Christianity and Social Progress* (*Mater et Magistra* - MM). This encyclical was pivotal to the emergence of a new paradigm in Catholic social doctrine.

After reviewing key elements in the teaching of his predecessors, Pope John analyzed the impact of modernization on people and concluded that radically new problems confront nations. The disparity in the distribution of wealth and the lack of opportunity for the poor to advance socially were particularly disturbing to the pope.

John XXIII concluded that in order for the various sectors in society to achieve a just balance, economic development was essential. The development process should be initiated by civil government, but should not exclude participation by the poor themselves. Civil authorities, he wrote, should bear in mind that:

> *Citizens in less developed countries—in giving attention to economic and social affairs, as well as in cultural matters—feel themselves to be the ones chiefly responsible for their own progress. For a citizen has a sense of his own dignity when he contributes the major share to progress in his own affairs.*
>
> *Hence, those who rely on their own resources and initiative should contribute as best they can to the equitable adjustment of economic life in their own community.* (MM: 151-152)

Although Pope John held an overly optimistic view of the benefits that would be derived from economic development, he brought a new awareness to the plight of the poor and the forces that caused their poverty. His understanding of the changing world was a catalyst for moving the church toward a new understanding of mission and a disengagement from alliances with the traditional structures that marginalized the poor and needy.

Vatican II

IT IS COMMONLY SAID that when Pope John XXIII convened the Second Vatican Council (October 1962), the windows of the church were indeed opened to the fresh air of the modern world. It was a *kairos* event in the history of the church. Among Catholics there is little disagreement that it marked the closing of the old era and the ushering in of a new (Henriot, DeBerri, Schultheis: 9).

The sixteen documents of Vatican II (released in 1964 and 1965) suggest that the Council Fathers were concerned with three broad, but interlocking, themes: 1) the need for doctrinal renewal which was centered around the Word of God and the mission of Christ; 2) institutional changes to modernize church structures; and 3) articulation of the church's response to the world's problems. The bishops effectively forged a new relationship between faith and justice.

Identifying the mission of the church

A number of documents contributed to reshaping the church's understanding of mission. *Dogmatic Constitution on the Church* (*Lumen Gentium* - LG) was the first to be drafted and provided the foundation for much of the creative work that followed. It identified the mission of the church with Jesus' being sent by the Father to bring the Good News to the poor. Therefore, in a special way, the church

> *is called to follow the same path if she is to communicate the fruits of salvation to men. Christ Jesus, "though he was by nature God . . . emptied himself, taking the nature of a slave" and "being rich, became poor" for our sake. Likewise, the*

> *church, although she needs human resources to carry out her mission, is not set up to seek earthly glory, but to proclaim, and this by her own example, humility and self-denial. Christ was sent by the Father "to bring good news to the poor . . . to heal the contrite of heart" . . . to "seek and save what was lost." Similarly, the church encompasses with her love all those who are afflicted by human misery and she recognizes in those who are poor and who suffer, the image of her poor and suffering founder. She does all in her power to relieve their need and in them she strives to serve Christ.* (LG: 8)

Sections 16 and 17 provide important teaching on the relationship of the church to the non-Christian world, thus providing a framework for the missionary nature of the church.

Overall, *Lumen Gentium* intentionally went beyond post-Tridentine ecclesiology—a clerical and imperialistic church. Instead, the church is presented as a humble, servant community. Ecclesiology was given missionary character. For theologian David Bosch, this was the real breakthrough in respect to mission (Bosch: 371-372).

The *Decree on Ecumenism* (*Unitatis Redintegratio* - UR) broke new ground in that the Vatican officially recognized the role of other Christian communions in the universal mission of the church. The imagery suggests a pilgrim church moving towards Christ whose spirit is at work beyond the visible bounds of the Catholic church.

Therefore, all Christians are called to work and pray for unity, to engage in dialogue and to cooperate for the common good, especially in matters concerned with social action and the promotion of justice. Such cooperation should "use every possible means to relieve the affliction of our times, such as famine and natural disasters, illiteracy and poverty, lack of housing, and the unequal distribution of wealth" (UR: 12). *Unitatis Redintegratio* was a powerful stimulus for revitalizing the ecumenical movement in general, and especially for cooperation in ministries of transformation.

A theological rationale for evangelization

In the *Decree on the Church's Missionary Activity* (*Ad Gentes* - AG), Council participants probed more deeply into the missionary nature of the church. This important document outlined a fresh perspective for thinking about mission.

1. Missionary work is not limited to work among non-Christian peoples. It calls for a new missionary thrust among baptized people in countries that are already evangelized (AG: 6).
2. Ecumenical cooperation in missionary work is essential. *Ad Gentes* points out that "the division of Christians is injurious to the holy work of preaching the Gospel to every creature, and deprives many people of access to faith" (AG: 6; see also AG: 15, 29, 36 and 41).
3. The missionary task challenges the church to "implant" itself among people groups that have not heard or responded to the gospel (AG: 10).
4. Christian witness in society is an important dimension of the missionary task (AG: 11).
5. The church is called to identify in a special way with the poor through witness in service and a ministry of love (AG: 12).
6. Human transformation is the goal of evangelization (AG: 13).

The influence of more progressive theologians, particularly Karl Rahner and Edward Schillebeeckx, is seen in AG: 9 which provides the theological rationale for evangelization among non-Christian peoples. This section says, in part,

> *Through preaching and the celebration of the sacraments . . . missionary activity makes Christ present, he who is the author of salvation. It purges of evil associations those elements of truth and grace which are found among peoples . . . as it were, a secret presence of God, and it restores them to Christ their source who overthrows the rule of the devil and limits the manifold malice of evil. So whatever goodness is found in the minds and hearts of men, or in the particular customs and cultures of peoples, far from being lost is purified, raised to a higher level and reaches its perfection, for the glory of God, the confusion of the demon, and the happiness of men.* (AG: 9)

The way in which this section is interpreted and applied is a source of ongoing debate within the church. We will return to this problem later.

The last of the Vatican II documents is the *Pastoral Constitution on the Church in the Modern World* (*Gaudium et Spes* - GS). It is the longest and, because of the variety and complexity of the issues addressed by the bishops, probably the most difficult document to understand. An important feature is its frequent appeal to Scripture to illumine issues under consideration. Overall, despite heated debate between conservatives and progressives during the drafting, *Gaudium et Spes* is a powerful statement by the church on its duty to enhance human dignity and on the universality and finality of Jesus Christ as Savior and Lord of history.

In one sense *Gaudium et Spes* provided little original thinking on development. Nevertheless, it contributed to the broad holistic theme in several important respects.

1. By affirming and restating previous teaching, the Council legitimized the shift already underway.
2. As the final statement, *Gaudium et Spes* established a climate in which broad principles could be contextualized in particular churches, and it smoothed the way for the creative changes which followed the conclusion of Vatican II. It gave a new perspective on "the world" and challenged the church to a truly new way of thinking.
3. Drafters recognized the limitations of using economic progress as the principal indicator to measure alleviation of poverty and injustice. They correctly saw that meaningful social and economic change required "a change of mentality and attitudes" among both rich and poor. This opened the way for more attention to values transformation in the development process (see GS: 63, 64, 86d).

Moving to a new openness

One of the most insightful assessments of Vatican II is provided by the Irish missionary priest and theologian, Donal Dorr. He suggests that *Gaudium et Spes* moved the church from a conservative to a liberal agenda. He defines the liberal agenda as a new openness both internally and externally—acceptance of pluralism as a fact in modern society and a corresponding willingness to interact with all who seek to make the world a more humane place in which to live. He believes the liberal agenda is the necessary precursor to a prophetic agenda, which frees the church to fulfill its ultimate role. The prophetic church serves the world, not by seeking consensus through balancing the competing interests of the liberal agenda. Rather, it challenges the world's value system. For Dorr, the church must be committed

> *not to the present world but the future—or, the present insofar as it is open to a very different and better future. It is not the world of the rich and powerful, or more accurately not the world as structured to favor the privileged groups. It is primarily a world of the dominated, the oppressed, the poor—a world in need of liberation.* (Dorr: 136-137)

The Second Vatican Council prepared the way for the integration of the development and evangelization strands in Catholic social teaching. Fr. Avery Dulles, well-known Jesuit theologian, believes the extensive use of "evangelical terminology" was indicative of a changing attitude towards evangelization. He points out that in contrast to the first Vatican Council, where the term "gospel" is used only once, Vatican II refers to the "gospel" 137 times, "evangelize" 18 times and "evangelization" 31 times. Moreover, the contexts in which the terms are used show that the Council Fathers meant proclamation of the Good News to those who have not yet believed in Jesus Christ (Dulles: 53).

This decisive shift opened the door to the articulation of a new vision in which evangelization would redefine the mission of the church. Dulles calls this "evangelization turn" one of the most surprising and important developments in the Catholic church in the post-Vatican II period (Dulles: 70).

The pontificate of Paul VI

THE PROPHETIC AGENDA of Donal Dorr was very evident during the fifteen-year pontificate of Paul VI, who encouraged forces in the church that were seeking greater identification of the church with the poor and oppressed. Msgr. Joseph Gremillion regards Pope Paul as being "determined and decisive" in his support of renewal elements, "thereby permitting the penetration of the *aggiornamento* [modernization] seminal convictions for a loving, serving church into the key structures of ecclesial community and ministry" (Gremillion: 138).

Pope Paul's encyclicals formulated bold principles, providing the framework for fresh pastoral responses to the problem of poverty and injustice. At the same time, the need for personal conversion permeated his vision for a transformed society—a holistic response to human need.

Paul VI's vision for Christian development

The first of Pope Paul's important pronouncements on justice and evangelization, *On the Development of Peoples* (*Populorum Progressio* - PP) was issued in 1967, sixteen months after he closed Vatican II. This encyclical presents his vision for Christian development. He rejects the view that development is economic growth (PP: 14). Rather, it derives from properly relating to God.

Human development is envisioned as a process in which people realize the potential given to them by God (PP: 15). External influences may aid or impede the process, but true development is possible only when people choose to "orientate their lives to God. . . . By reason of his union with Christ, the source of life, man attains to a new fulfillment of himself, to a transcendent humanism which gives his greatest possible perfection: this is the highest goal of personal development" (PP: 16).

O'Brien and Shannon interpret Pope Paul's "transcendent humanism" to mean human maturity which is continually open to growth (O'Brien and Shannon: 309). For this reason it is appropriate for individuals to "seek to do more, know more and have more in order to be more" (PP: 6).

Two additional points are vital to Pope Paul's vision of development. First, because individuals form part of a social unit, development takes place in a community where all are called to the fullness of development (PP: 17). Therefore, development is communal in nature. Second, values are central to the growth process. Wherever the "true scale of values" is undermined, development in both the personal and communal aspects is threatened.

Paul VI sounded a warning about preoccupation with the desire for material goods because it leads to greed, to the "insatiable desire for more and more" and makes power a "tempting objective" (PP: 18). For him, the erosion of values is the most blatant form of moral underdevelopment, and greed is its most prominent manifestation (PP: 19). In his vision, in order for development to be authentic "it must be complete . . . it has to promote the good of every man and of the whole man" (PP: 14).

Integrating theology with social action

The Medellín Conference of the Latin American bishops convened in 1968, a year after *Populorum Progressio*. The conference was an intentional effort to apply church social teaching to the specific context of poverty and injustice in Latin America. In so doing, the bishops tried to integrate biblical theology with practical social action. Transformation, they insist, is grounded in the gospel.

> *The uniqueness of the Christian message does not so much consist in the affirmation of the necessity for structural change, as it does in the insistence on conversion of men which in turn brings about this change. We will not have a new continent without new and reformed structures, but, above all, there will be no new continent without new men, who know how to be truly free and responsible according to the light of the Gospel.* (MD: J3).

Also, affirmation by the bishops of the importance of small Christian communities in bringing marginalized people to participate in political and economic processes validated an increasingly popular way to form and equip laity for ministry. Conscientizing would become a powerful tool in the church's efforts to effect reformation of structures (MD: J20).

The next milestone occurs in 1971. The document entitled *Justice in the World* (JW) summarized the work of the 1971 Synod of Bishops. It is a "strong, positive document sanctioned by papal and episcopal approval . . . to give powerful support to those in all nations working to bring the church into a more active, vigilant and pastoral relationship to the problems of peace and justice" (O'Brien and Shannon: 384).

Basically, the bishops clarified, and in some instances expanded, the work of Medellín. For example, they devoted an entire chapter (JW: 29-38) to "The Gospel Message and the Mission of the Church." They challenged the view that rapid economic growth was the panacea for the ills of poverty and concluded that marginalized people themselves must be part of the process to remove structured injustice. People in oppressive societies must first be formed Christianly so that Christian values will permeate the struggle for justice.

Therefore, Christian formation is an essential part of the development process (JW: 49). To be formed Christianly entails "a renewal of heart . . . based on the recognition of sin in its individual and social manifestations." A "critical sense" will be awakened, leading to reflection on societal values. Values that do not promote justice and contribute to human development will be rejected (JW: 51). A value change in the life of people affected by poverty and injustice is integral to transformation.

Echoing Vatican II on the importance of ecumenical cooperation, the bishops conclude that collaboration in development should include the teaching of the gospel, so long as it flows from the mission of the universal church rather than from partisan or sectarian motives (JW: 61).

The most significant debate resulted from action by the bishops to nullify a dualistic understanding of the church's mission. They declared that "action on behalf of justice and participation in the transformation of the world fully appear to us as a *constitutive dimension* [italics added] of the preaching of the gospel, or, in other words, of the church's mission for the redemption of the human race and its liberation from every oppressive situation" (JW: 6).

The bishops' statement sparked a storm of controversy. The commonly accepted interpretation is that the Synod Fathers understood action to promote justice and development to be an *essential* part of carrying out the church's mission.

This was contrary to traditionalists who contend that the mission of the church is basically spiritual or religious. This group regards social action as secular activity, hence of secondary importance to the work of evangelization. In their view "constitutive" should be understood as meaning "important." Dorr insists, however, that the 1971 Synod wished to insure that social and political action would always be central to the church's mission, rather than being dismissed as irrelevant or relegated to a peripheral role (see Dorr: 187-189).

Evangelization and transformation

The controversy over use of the term "constitutive dimension" was probably in Pope Paul's mind when he chose the evangelization of the modern world as the theme for the Synod of Bishops in 1974. Although it was widely assumed that the bishops would reconcile conflicting points of view on the church's prophetic role, they were unable to do so. Consequently, the bishops requested the pope to issue a document on this important issue. A year later, in 1975, he released the landmark *Evangelization in the Modern World* (*Evangelii Nuntiandi* - EN).

In his introduction, Pope Paul posed the three "burning questions" the 1974 synod had kept in mind:

- In our day, what has happened to the hidden energy of the Good News that is able to have a powerful effect on man's conscience?
- To what extent and in what way is that evangelical force capable of really transforming the people of this century?
- What methods should be followed so that the power of the gospel may have its full effect (EN: 4)?

The three questions point to the fundamental issue facing the church. In the aftermath of Vatican II, ". . . does the church or does she not find herself better equipped to proclaim the Gospel and to put it into people's hearts with conviction, freedom of spirit and effectiveness" (EN: 4)?

The pope considers his exhortation to be "of capital importance" because

> *the presentation of the gospel message is not an optional contribution for the church. It is the duty incumbent upon her by the command of the Lord Jesus, so that people can believe and be saved. This message is indeed necessary. It is unique. It cannot be replaced. It does not permit either indifference, syncretism or accommodation. It is a question of people's salvation.* (EN: 5)

Throughout this apostolic exhortation, Pope Paul brings the weight of biblical theology and pastoral experience to fashion his response to problems of justice and transformation. Although there is a great deal of overlap, we can identify three main themes in *Evangelii Nuntiandi*.

The first theme treats the relation of the kingdom of God to evangelization.

> *As an evangelizer, Christ first of all proclaims a Kingdom, the Kingdom of God; and this is so important that, by comparison everything else becomes "the rest" which is given in addition. Only the Kingdom therefore is absolute, and it makes everything else relative.* (EN: 8)

Because the kingdom is central, the church is not an end unto itself. It is a community of believers responding in obedience to Jesus' command to go out into the world and proclaim the gospel. The kingdom community is an evangelizing community (EN: 13).

The kingdom is not an abstraction, Pope Paul asserts. It demands a new manner of being and living. It is concerned with transforming "both the personal and collective consciences of people, the activities in which they engage, and the lives and concrete milieux which are theirs" (EN: 18).

Pre-eminently, the kingdom is incarnated in the community of the transformed faithful (EN: 23).

In the second theme the pope looked at evangelization as process. He envisioned a society that is transformed by the power of the gospel which impacts values, decision-making, motivation and lifestyle (EN: 19). Therefore, evangelization considers the interplay between the gospel and a person's daily life in its personal and social dimensions (EN: 29).

The pope recognized that rigid methodologies will impede this process. Therefore, methods must vary according to circumstances, such as "time, place and culture." He urged the bishops to reshape "with boldness and wisdom, but in complete fidelity to the content of evangelization" the means that are best suited to communicate the gospel to women and men in the contemporary world (EN: 40).

The content, or message, in evangelization is communicated through life's witness and verbal proclamation. "The first means of evangelization is the witness of authentic Christian living, given over to God in a communion that nothing should destroy, and at the same time given to one's neighbor in limitless zeal" (EN: 41). However, "the Good News proclaimed by the witness of life must sooner or later lead to the proclamation of the Word of Life. There is no true evangelization if the Name, the teaching, the life, the promise of the kingdom, and the mystery of Jesus of Nazareth, the Son of God, are not proclaimed" (EN: 22).

Pope Paul did not assign relative importance to witness on the one hand and proclamation on the other. Rather, he argued that both are of fundamental importance but in different ways. Witness without words may be opaque to the secular mind. But it is also true that words without the witness of consecrated Christian living lack credibility in the modern world.

Paul VI acknowledged that evangelization is a complex process composed of seemingly contradictory elements—"renewal of humanity, witness, explicit proclamation, inner adherence, entry into the community, acceptance of signs, apostolic initiative" (EN: 24). Actually, these elements are complementary and mutually enriching because all are needed to evangelize persons and their respective cultures. For Pope Paul the relationship is clear.

> *All this could be expressed in the following words: What matters is to evangelize man's culture and cultures (not in a purely decorative way as it were by applying a thin veneer, but in a vital way, in depth and right to their very roots), . . . always taking the person as one's starting point and always coming back to the relationships of people among themselves and with God. . . . Though independent of cultures, the Gospel and evangelization are not necessarily incompatible with them; rather they are capable of permeating them all without becoming subject to any one of them. Therefore, every effort must be made to ensure a full evangelization of culture. . . . They have to be regenerated by an encounter with the Gospel. But this encounter will not take place if the Gospel is not proclaimed.* (EN: 20)

A proper understanding of liberation

Liberation is the third major theme in *Evangelii Nuntiandi*. The concept was being used increasingly as a synonym for salvation. Consequently, social activists tended to equate political activity—liberating the poor from oppressive structures—with evangelization. In his apostolic exhortation Pope Paul sought to clarify the church's teaching on this volatile issue.

First, he addressed the need to articulate a proper understanding of liberation. He argued that the concept derives its meaning from the gospel message—the proclamation of a salvation which liberates men and women from every oppressive thing, and pre-eminently from sin and Satan (EN: 9). Because this liberation was already accomplished by Christ on the cross and authenticated in his resurrection, to focus on structural reform would divert the church from her central mission.

Therefore, the transformation of values resulting from a personal encounter with Christ takes precedence over systemic renewal. He reasons that while the church does not diminish the need to reshape structures to make them "more human, more just, more respectful of the rights of the person and less oppressive and less enslaving," the reality is that even the most ideal structures are shaped by sinful humanity unless those who rule them "undergo a conversion of heart and of outlook" (EN: 36).

For this reason, the church's mission cannot be reduced to purely temporal methods that equate economic and political well-being with salvation. Such an approach would strip the church of her "fundamental meaning," leaving her prey to sectarian ideologies. To counter this way of thinking, Pope Paul asserted the "specifically religious finality of evangelization," which is guided by the axis of the kingdom of God (EN: 32).

> *When preaching liberation and associating herself with those who are working and suffering for it, the church is certainly not willing to restrict her*

> *mission only to the religious field and dissociate herself from man's temporal problems. Nevertheless she affirms the primacy of her spiritual vocation and refuses to replace the proclamation of the kingdom by the proclamation of forms of human liberation; she even states that her contribution to liberation is incomplete if she neglects to proclaim salvation in Jesus Christ.* (EN: 34)

Having defined liberation in terms of the gospel impertive, Paul VI then acknowledges the "profound" link between evangelization and liberation. The link is anthropological ("because the man who is to be evangelized is not an abstract being but is subject to social and economic questions") and theological ("since one cannot dissociate the plan of creation from the plan of redemption").

Because of these links it is impossible that evangelization "could or should" ignore problems concerned with justice, liberation and development. "This would be to forget the lesson which comes to us from the Gospel concerning love of our neighbor who is suffering and in need" (EN: 31).

The impact of *Evangelii Nuntiandi*

Even in disagreement, few question the profound impact of *Evangelii Nuntiandi* on Catholic thought and practice, both for evangelization and the broader ministry of transformation. Fr. John Walsh provides a good assessment.

> *What we observe is a further dissolution of the body-soul dichotomy that plagued the ministry for so long. Body-soul may be a good distinction in certain forms of theology but unfortunately it has often become a dichotomy when transferred to actual ministry: sacred versus secular, eternal ver-*

> *sus time, spiritual versus material. Now, we are closer to the mind-set of Christ as found in Scripture. . . . The person is a totality; an embodied person, a personalized body, a body-person. And one ministers to the whole person. The church is in the process of reaffirming this most important scriptural insight when it states that human development, liberation, justice and peace are integral parts of the ministry of evangelization.* (Walsh: 91-92)

Viewing it from a somewhat different perspective, Dorr comments:

> *Despite elements of incompleteness in the way in which* Evangelii Nuntiandi *treats the issue of liberation and the role of the church in promoting it . . . the document makes a very significant contribution towards a better understanding of this whole question. . . .* Rerum Novarum *was important, not so much because of its content as because it represented a decisive intervention by the pope on behalf of the poor.* Evangelii Nuntiandi, *on the other hand, is important in relation to the poor for precisely the opposite reason. Some of the content of the document is exceptionally important in enabling Christians to know how the deepest roots of poverty and oppression can be overcome.* (Dorr: 205-206)

John Paul II

AFTER HIS ELECTION, Pope John Paul II approved the convening of the Third General Conference of Latin American bishops. There was considerable speculation about the new pope's position on the progressive direction taken by the church since Vatican II. Conservative bishops controlled the important preparatory work leading to the Puebla (Mexico) Conference. Consequently, many observers felt that the Puebla Conference would undo what had been achieved at Medellín ten years earlier. The new pope's role would be crucial to the outcome.

Development and evangelization

The Puebla Conference met in January 1979. Basically, it explored the interplay between development and evangelization in the church's mission. The report is lengthy and in some instances ambiguous. It is generally felt that Pope John Paul's influence was instrumental in reconciling competing views and interests.

Conservatives were heartened by the affirmation of biblical orthodoxy as the starting place for formulating a response to issues of poverty and justice. The bishops rejected a non-Christian view of liberation, relying heavily on Paul VI's *Evangelii Nuntiandi*. "We mutilate liberation in an unpardonable way if we do not achieve liberation from sin . . . and if we do not help to make concrete the liberation that Christ won on the cross" (PD: 485). Therefore, in God's plan for humankind the person of Jesus must not be distorted, factionalized or idealized (PD: 178).

At the same time, the pastoral response to Latin America's problems applied the biblical principles in a manner that also addressed concerns shared by progressive and moderate bishops. The Puebla Document calls for radical discipleship and a love that gives a privileged place to the poor (PD: 192-193). Evangelization, which should penetrate deeply into the hearts of individuals, aims at both personal conversion and social transformation (PD: 362). The bishops acclaimed the importance of basic ecclesial communities for embodying the church's "preferential option" for the poor (PD: 629).

Despite criticism from radical factions, there is broad consensus that Puebla moved the church forward rather than backward. An influential moderate, Archbishop McGrath of Panama, summed up results as

> *a conscious step to break the dichotomy between theology and social action, between faith and life. The social teaching of the church as presented by Puebla is the fruit of theological-pastoral reflection on the social stirrings of Christians. It involves the whole church and its life situation. It expands, applies and adopts according to the changing circumstances of time and place, in constant fidelity to the gospel.* (Eagleson and Scharper: 100)

Reacting to charges by critics that Puebla moved away from Medellín, Dom Helder Camara of Brazil responded, "as bishops, we have not betrayed our people, but on the contrary, with divine grace, have been able to carry forward the strength of Medellín" (Eagleson and Scharper: 41).

Most importantly, Puebla demonstrated continued papal support for the process set in motion by Vatican II. In an address to the bishops, John Paul said, "If the church gets involved in promoting or defending human dignity, it does so in accordance with its mission. For even though the mission is religious in character, and not social or political, it cannot help but consider human persons in terms of their whole being. . . . The church has learned that an indispensable part of its evangelizing mission is made up of works on behalf of justice and human promotion" (Opening Address III: 2).

The pope issued his first encyclical in 1979, shortly after Puebla, with the title *Redeemer of Man* (*Redemptor Hominis* - RH). The encyclical was dedicated to exploring the relationship between the mystery of redemption in Jesus Christ and the dignity of man.

The two-fold theme—persons as created by God, and persons as being redeemed by Christ—would be the hallmark of John Paul's pontificate and is central to his understanding of the church's mission. On the occasion of the release of *Redemptor Hominis* he commented, "As I see and feel the relationship of the mystery of redemption in Christ and the dignity of man, so would I want to unite the mission of the church with service to man, in this impenetrable mystery" (*Catholic International*: Vol 2, No. 6:254).

A strong Christology provides the framework for John Paul's redemptive theme. "It is in Christ and through Christ that persons become more fully aware of their own dignity, which is the proper basis for human development" (RH: 11). To be truly human is to be in a living relationship with Christ (RH: 10; 12).

Consequently, "the church . . . regards this concern for human beings and their humanity, . . . for the entire course of developmental progress, as being an essential part of her mission and indissolubly connected with it. She finds her warranty for this concern in Jesus Christ, himself, as the gospels make clear" (RH: 15).

In 1987 Pope John Paul issued another encyclical to commemorate the twentieth anniversary of Paul VI's *Popu-*

lorum Progressio. *Social Concerns* (*Sollicitudo Rei Socialis* - SRS) asserts that development is essentially moral in character because it is primarily concerned with values that govern human relationships. Anything which impedes the development of people expresses a negative value. These values stem from both personal and structural sin. He points out that structures are products of the individuals who shape and maintain them. If left unattended, these structures grow stronger, become more diffuse in society and profoundly influence people's behavior (SRS: 33-36).

Because authentic human development is measured in moral terms, forms of development that do not include cultural and religious dimensions of humanity in society are not really conducive to the liberation of the poor (SRS: 46). He proposes that the way to peace and development lies in solidarity, which he defines as "love and service of neighbors, especially of the poorest" (SRS: 46).

Both development and liberation are concretized when solidarity in relationships is maintained. It leads to sharing of goods and services by the powerful with the weak, while the powerless will strive to claim their legitimate rights. Because solidarity is a Christian virtue, the church is called to stand with the poor in the interest of justice and the common good (SRS: 39-40).

The nature of the church's holistic mission

Throughout his pontificate, John Paul has shown deep concern about more radical interpretations of the church's mission, particularly as expressed in certain theologies of liberation and missiological approaches that diminish the role of traditional missionary activity.

In response to this persistent problem, the pope issued another encyclical, entitled *The Redeemer's Mission*

(*Redemptoris Missio* - RM). Issued in December 1990, this is the most important missiological pronouncement since *Evangelii Nuntiandi*.

Redemptoris Missio defines the problem by posing a series of questions.

> *. . . as a result of the changes which have taken place in modern times and the spread of new theological ideas, some people wonder: is missionary work among non-Christians still relevant? Has it not been replaced by interreligious dialogue? Is not human development an adequate goal of the church's mission? Does not respect for conscience and for freedom exclude all efforts at conversion? Is it not possible to attain salvation in any religion? Why then should there be missionary activity?* (RM: 4)

If we conclude that Vatican II opened the door to theologies of witness and liberation and challenged traditional Christology, then *Redemptoris Missio* appears to be a clear attempt to provide corrective instruction on the nature of the church's holistic mission. The pope confronts the problem head on. To those who would ask, "Why mission?" he responds:

> *We reply with the church's faith and experience that true liberation consists in opening oneself to the love of Christ. In him, and only in him, are we set free from all alienation and doubt, from slavery to the power of sin and death. Christ is truly our peace; the love of Christ impels us, giving meaning and joy to our life. Mission is an issue of faith, an accurate indication of our faith in Christ*

> *and his love for us. . . . The temptation today is to reduce Christianity to merely human wisdom, a pseudoscience of well-being. In our heavily secularized world a gradual 'secularization of salvation' has taken place, so that people strive for the good of man, but man who is truncated, reduced to his merely horizontal dimension. We know, however, that Jesus came to bring integral salvation, one which embraces the whole person and all mankind and opens up wondrous prospects of divine filiation. . . . Why mission? Because to us as to Paul, "this grace was given to preach to the Gentiles the unsearchable riches of Christ." Newness of life in him is the good news for men and women in every age: all are called to it. . . . Indeed, all people are searching for it, albeit at times in a confused way, and have a right to know the value of this gift to approach it freely.* (RM: 11)

The themes of *Redemptoris Missio*

Redemptoris Missio is wordy. Some of its language is not easily understood. However, six themes are prominent.

First, the kingdom of God is the aim of mission. John Paul rejects the "anthropocentric" orientation of certain types of liberation theology that distort the meaning of the kingdom. He writes, "There are ideas about mission and salvation which can be called 'anthropocentric' . . . inasmuch as they are focused on man's earthly needs. In this view the kingdom tended to become something completely human and secularized: what counts are programs and struggles for a liberation which is social and economic, political and even cultural, but with a horizon that is closed to the transcendent. . . . Such a view translates into one more ideology of purely earthly progress. The kingdom of God, however, is not of this world" (RM: 17).

The encyclical enunciates a set of propositions that maintain the centrality of the kingdom to the church's holistic mission.

1. The kingdom is at the heart of evangelization because it cannot be detached from the person and work of Christ. Jesus proclaimed the kingdom and in his person the kingdom was present (RM: 13).
2. Christ's encounters with Gentiles is a clear indication that, while the kingdom is open to all, entry into it comes through faith and conversion (RM: 13).
3. The Good News of the kingdom has special relevance for society's poor and marginalized (RM: 14).
4. The kingdom offers salvation that is both physical and spiritual (RM: 14).
5. The kingdom is concerned with transformation of relationships (RM: 15).
6. Participation in building the kingdom means working for liberation from evil in its various forms (RM: 15).
7. The kingdom demands both the promotion of human values and values the pope calls "evangelical" (proclaiming Christ and his gospel) in an integrated way (RM: 19).
8. The church is the servant of the kingdom (RM: 20).

A second theme reflects on the continuing validity of mission *ad gentes* (to the nations).

John Paul feels the need to reaffirm mission to the nations because of the apparent waning in missionary activity which, he states, is not in line with the directives of Vatican II and subsequent pronouncements by the magisterium (teaching authority). "Difficulties both internal and external have weakened the church's missionary thrust towards non-Christians, a fact which must arouse concern among all who believe in Christ. For in the church's history, missionary drive has always been a sign of vitality, just as its lessening is a sign of crisis of faith" (RM: 1).

While acknowledging the universal nature of missionary activity and the need for re-evangelization of traditional Christian countries, he insists that mission is still preeminently carried out in defined geographical areas among specific groups of people (RM: 37). Also, there is a sociological dimension: the challenge of urbanization, the displacement of millions of people who are migrants and refugees, and the challenge of alienated youth.

The pope concludes that, "The mission *ad gentes* is still in its infancy. New people appear on the world scene, and they too have a right to receive the proclamation of salvation. Population growth in the non-Christian countries of South and East is constantly increasing the number of people who remain unaware of Christ's redemption. We need therefore to direct our attention towards these geographical areas and cultural settings which still remain uninfluenced by the gospel" (RM: 40).

Third, the pope speaks to forms of mission, particularly the interplay between witness and proclamation. Although witness is the "first form of evangelization," proclamation is its permanent priority. Witness entails living out kingdom values in daily life. The presence of kingdom values, especially as they imitate Jesus in his concern for the poor, the weak, the oppressed, and those who suffer, raise questions that point people towards God and the Good News (RM: 42).

On the other hand, "Evangelization will always contain—as the foundation, center and at the same time the summit of its dynamism—a clear proclamation that in

Jesus Christ . . . salvation is offered to all men as a gift of God's grace and mercy" (RM: 44). The goal of proclamation is conversion, which is "a complete and sincere adherence to Christ and his gospel through faith" (RM: 46).

John Paul dismisses missiological views that consider proclamation and conversion to be proselytism. It is not enough, he asserts, "to help people become more human or more faithful to their own religion," or "to build more communities capable of working for justice, freedom, peace and solidarity." These approaches overlook the right of all people to hear the gospel and respond to its invitation (RM: 46).

A fourth area is inculturation, which is defined as "the intimate transformation of authentic cultural values through their integration in Christianity and the insertion of Christianity in the various human cultures" (RM: 52). Inculturation is a lengthy process, but it must not compromise the uniqueness and integrity of the Christian faith (RM: 52).

To illustrate this point, the pope cites the Apostle Paul's experience in Athens (Acts 17:22-34). As a missionary Paul demonstrated understanding of and sensitivity to Athenian cultural and religious values, and even acknowledged the already existing presence of the God whom Paul wished to reveal. However, for the Athenians to be in relationship with the true God required abandoning their idols (false gods), repentance, and opening themselves to God's Son who alone could dispel their ignorance and satisfy the longing in their hearts (RM: 25).

Fifth, he addresses the need to promote "integral development and liberation." He refers to Puebla and various papal statements to affirm the role of missionaries in promoting development among the people they serve. At the same time, he cautions that the church does not have technical solutions for the problem of underdevelopment. Rather, the church's mission consists in "offering people an opportunity not to have more but to be more, by awakening their consciences through the gospel. Authentic human development must be rooted in evangelization" (RM: 58). Again,

> *Through the gospel message, the church offers a force for liberation which promotes development precisely because it leads to conversion of heart and of ways of thinking, fosters the recognition of each person's dignity, encourages solidarity, commitment and service of one's neighbors, and gives everyone a place in God's plan which is the building of his kingdom. . . . Man's development derives from God, from the model of Jesus . . . that is why there is a close connection between the proclamation of the gospel and human promotion.* (RM: 59)

Finally, John Paul looks to the Holy Spirit who "is indeed the principal agent of the whole of the church's mission" (RM: 21). He carefully examines the New Testament to understand the role and ministry of the Spirit in earliest church history and concludes that the Spirit both directs the church's mission and forms it as a community of believers (RM: 24; 26). But his activity is not limited to the church. The Spirit is present and active in time and space. He works in various cultures sowing "seeds of the Word," "preparing them for full maturity in Christ" (RM: 28).

The pope is careful to point out, though, that "whatever the Spirit brings about in human hearts and in the history of peoples, in cultures and religions serves as a preparation for the gospel and can only be understood in reference to Christ, the Word who took flesh by the power of the Spirit so that as perfectly human he would save all human beings and sum up all things" (RM: 29).

The "new evangelization"

The themes expounded by John Paul in *Redemptoris Missio* are not new. He draws from Vatican II and Paul VI's *Evangelii Nuntiandi*. This approach is consistent with his desire to maintain continuity while insuring that renewal opens new doors of opportunity in the rapidly changing world (SRS: 3).

More recently, at the opening of the Fourth General Assembly of the Latin American bishops, John Paul reminded the bishops that the task facing the church today "is to make the truth about Christ and the truth about mankind penetrate more deeply into all strata of society and transform them" (*The Pope Speaks*: 87).

Reflecting on his call for the new evangelization, the pope was careful to point out that it does not consist of a new message, a "gospel" arising "from us, from our culture, or our analyses of the needs of mankind." Such a message would be "mere human invention, and salvation would not be found in it." Challenging some contemporary views about inculturation, he insisted that the new evangelization does not mean "removing from the Gospel whatever seems difficult for the modern mentality to accept" (*The Pope Speaks*: 87).

Rather, the point of departure for the new evangelization is the "certitude that in Christ there are 'inscrutable riches' (Eph. 3:8) which no culture nor era can exhaust, and which we must bring to people in order to enrich them. These riches are, first of all, Christ himself, His person, because He Himself is our salvation" (*The Pope Speaks*: 88).

"Therefore," the pope declared,

> *the Gospel must be preached in total fidelity and purity, as it has been preserved and handed on by*

> *the Church's Tradition. Evangelizing means proclaiming a person, Christ. Indeed, "there is no true evangelization if the name, the teaching, the life, the kingdom and the mystery of Jesus of Nazareth, the Son of God, are not proclaimed. Therefore, reductive Christologies . . . are unacceptable as tools of the new evangelization.* (The Pope Speaks: 88)

It is in the broad framework of evangelization that the church exercises its concern for the social order, which the pope insists "is part of the Church's evangelizing mission" because it is "an essential part of the Christian message." Therefore, "human development must be the logical consequence of evangelization, which aims at the total liberation of the human person" (*The Pope Speaks*: 91).

The church is entrusted with the task of heralding hope: "a hope that rests on the promises of God, in fidelity to His word and which has its unshakable certainty in the resurrection of Christ, His definitive victory over sin and death, the first proclamation and the root of all evangelization, the foundation of all human development, the principle of all authentic Christian culture . . . inspired by the breath of the Spirit of Pentecost" (*The Pope Speaks*: 98).

Theologian Avery Dulles considers the "evangelical turn" of Paul VI and John Paul II to be one of the most surprising developments in the post-Vatican II church. Its significance is underscored by the fact that while both popes broadened the concept of evangelization to include human transformation, they have retained what Dulles considers the "kerygmatic essence" of evangelization. He writes:

> *For centuries evangelization had been a poor stepchild. Even when the term was used, evangelization was treated as a secondary matter, the*

special vocation of a few priests and religious. Even these specialists were more concerned with gaining new adherents for the church than with proclaiming the Good News of Jesus Christ. Today we seem to be witnessing the birth of a new catholicism which, without loss of its institutional, sacramental and social dimensions, is authentically evangelical. (Dulles: 70)

The response to the new direction

Dulles supports the view that, in general, Catholic bishops have responded positively to the direction charted by the post-conciliar popes. In the Philippines, for example, the 1991 Plenary Council II approved recommendations that will make evangelization the cornerstone of diocesan pastoral ministry for the next decade.

The 1991 Special Assembly for Europe of the Synod of Bishops, represented by 21 bishops' conferences, acknowledged that for many persons today, particularly in the younger generation, the Christian faith is virtually unknown. The bishops concluded that "the Church's most urgent task is to proclaim anew to the people of Europe the liberating message of the Gospel" ("To Be Witnesses of Christ Who Has Set Us Free": 3).

The bishops in Zambia have identified three priorities for evangelization in that nation: the clear proclamation of Jesus Christ as Savior, inculturation of the message to make it authentically African, and ministries to promote integral development ("You Shall Be My Witnesses": 15, 20, 26).

A special Synod of Bishops for Africa will be held at the Vatican in 1994. Its theme is "The Church in Africa and Her Evangelizing Mission Towards the Year 2000: You Shall Be My Witnesses" (*Catholic Trends* [Feb.13, 1993],

Vol. 23, No. 15:2). In October 1992, Latin American bishops met in Santo Domingo for the Fourth General Conference of Latin American Bishops. They chose the theme "The New Evangelization, Human Development and Christian Culture."

One of the most dynamic responses is Evangelization 2000. With headquarters in Rome, six regional offices actively promote evangelization around the world. They have sponsored numerous retreats for bishops and priests and established a network of schools of evangelization. More than 400 contemplative monasteries and hundreds of prayer groups undergird the ministry of evangelization with around-the-clock intercession. Evangelization 2000 has captured the imagination of clergy and laity alike.

The "new evangelization" is not universally endorsed, as evidenced by the resistance expressed by some U.S. bishops. But current trends suggest that it is already rooted in the consciousness of the church. Avery Dulles concludes that "the popes of our time have correctly identified God's call to the church in our day." He continues:

> *Unless the Gospel message were a truth to be communicated to others, it would not be of great value for believers themselves. Once we grasp the universal validity of the message and its significance for the whole of human life, we gain a new appreciation of the privilege of being its bearers and a new eagerness to share it. Evangelization, by concentrating on the basic Christian message, helps to see what is supremely worthwhile in our religion. If we believe simply on the authority of the church, without caring what the contents are, we can hardly be enthusiastic about our faith. But if we focus on the God of Jesus Christ, as disclosed in*

the Gospel, our faith becomes a loving assent to an extraordinary piece of Good News intended for all the world. . . . In evangelizing we are required to raise our eyes to Him and transcend all ecclesio-centrism. The church is of crucial importance but it is not self-enclosed. It is the means of drawing the whole world into union with God through Jesus Christ. (Dulles: 71)

Implications for ministry and mission

SOME GENERAL CONCLUSIONS can be drawn from this study.

1. There is a broad area of convergence between Catholic teaching and the philosophy of ministry embraced by a number of evangelical development agencies. Such an approach features the centrality of the kingdom of God, God's special concern for the poor and the challenge of world evangelization.
2. The concept of development as transformation is embraced by both in their approaches to ministry. It derives from the biblical model of Jesus' concern for wholeness and fullness of life. Roman Catholic concern for a loving, serving church is parallel to the commitment by World Vision and others to servanthood in their ministry.
3. Roman Catholic concern for a loving, serving church is paralleled by an evangelical commitment to servanthood in ministry. World Vision, for example, has embodied such a commitment in the organization's statement of core values.
4. Although Roman Catholics and evangelicals use somewhat different language to describe the development process, there is broad agreement on the concept of empowerment as an effective means for people to transform their present reality into a better future.
5. Both Paul VI and John Paul II locate human development in the broader context of evangelization. Therefore, the transformation of society is grounded in God's salvific acts rather than in reliance on purely human effort. With evangelical belief, magisterial teaching rejects the tendency to dichotomize the

spiritual (evangelism) and the material-physical-secular (development). Both understand evangelization to include witness through word (proclamation) and deed (signs).

6. The post-Vatican II Catholic church affirms the continuing validity of the evangelization of peoples as being central to mission. Terms such as *evangelism* and *evangelization* carry subtle differences in understanding for Catholics and evangelicals. Nevertheless, papal teaching clearly stresses the imperative of sharing the gospel with those who have not heard and responded to its message.
7. Although we acknowledge differences in the way evangelicals and Protestants understand some theological and doctrinal issues, affirmation of a common call to share in Christ's mission in the world is not dependent on uniformity in all points of doctrine and liturgical practice. Among the important areas on which there is essential agreement are: a trinitarian understanding of God, Christology, and the belief that Scriptures provide the primary resource for forming Christians in their faith and shaping their value system.

The convergence in our understanding of holistic mission has important implications both for the way we think about ministry and the way in which cooperative programs might be structured.

At this period in history, the world is faced with unprecedented human need. The task facing the universal church is very great. Roman Catholic affirmation of the importance of ecumenical cooperation in responding to these needs is an encouraging sign. It demands a positive response from evangelicals.

Tapping the potential benefits resulting from broader contact and cooperation will require vision and courage to act. If this can be done, the resulting fellowship in witness and service will be powerful testimony to the lordship of Christ in the world and will demonstrate the unity for which our Lord prayed.

Bibliography

Bosch, David J. 1991. *Transforming Mission*. Maryknoll: Orbis Books.

Buhlmann, Walbert. 1978. *The Coming of the Third Church*. Maryknoll: Orbis Books.

Burrows, William R., SVD. "Tensions in the Catholic Magisterium About Mission and Other Religious." *International Bulletin of Missionary Research*, Volume 9, No. 1 (January 1985).

Catholic Bishops of Zambia. "'You Shall Be My Witnesses': A Second Century of Evangelization in Zambia." *Catholic International*, Volume 2, No. 17 (Oct. 1-14, 1991).

Curran, Charles E. and McCormic, Richard A., SJ, eds. 1986. *Official Catholic Social Teaching: Readings in Moral Theology, No. 5*. New York: Paulist Press.

De Achutegui, Pedro S., SJ. 1987. *Along the Pathways of the Council: 1987 Synod of Bishops*. Manila: Loyola School of Theology.

Dorr, Donal. 1983. *Option for the Poor*. Maryknoll: Orbis Books and revised edition (1992).

Dulles, Avery, SJ. "John Paul II and the New Evangelization." *America*, Volume 166, No. 3 (February 1, 1992).

Eagleson, John and Sharper, Philip, eds. 1979. *Puebla and Beyond*. Maryknoll: Orbis Books.

Europe Synod of Bishops. "Final Declaration: 'To Be Witnesses of Christ Who Has Set Us Free.'" *Catholic International*, Volume 3, No. 5 (March 1-14, 1992).

Ferguson, James J., C.S.C. "A Paradigm Shift in the Theology of Mission: Two Roman Catholic Perspectives." *International Bulletin of Missionary Research*, Volume 8, No. 3 (July 1984).

Flannery, Austin, O.P., ed. 1975 and 1984. *Vatican Council II:*

The Conciliar and Post Conciliar Documents. Maryknoll: Orbis Books.

Gremillion, Joseph, ed. 1978. *The Gospel of Peace and Justice: Catholic Social Teaching Since Pope John*. Maryknoll: Orbis Books.

Henriot, Peter J., DeBerri, Edward, and Schultheis, Michael J. 1989. *Catholic Social Teaching: Our Best Kept Secret*. Quezon City, Philippines: Claretian Publishers.

John XXIII. [1961]. "Mater et Magistra." *The Gospel of Peace and Justice*. Edited by Joseph Gremillion. Maryknoll: Orbis Books, 1976.

John Paul II. "Challenges Facing the Latin Church." *The Pope Speaks*, Volume 38, No. 2 (March-April 1993).

______. 1979. "Opening Address at the Puebla Conference." *Puebla and Beyond*. Edited by John Eagleson and Philip Scharper. Maryknoll: Orbis Books.

______. "Redemptor Hominis." *The Pope Speaks*, Volume 24, No. 3 (May-June 1979).

______. "Redemptoris Missio." *Catholic International*, Volume 2, No. 6 (March 1991).

______. "Social and Political Problems Are the Responsibility of the Whole Church." *The Pope Speaks*, Volume 37, No. 1 (January-February 1992).

______.1988. *Sollicitudo Rei Socialis*. Manila: Saint Paul Publications.

Knitter, Paul F. "Roman Catholic Approaches to Other Religions: Developments and Tensions." *International Bulletin of Missionary Research*, Volume 8, No. 2, (June 1984).

Kroeger, James H. "Many Faces and Challenges." *World Mission* (June 1990).

Latin America Bishops. [1968]. "Medellín Documents." *The Gospel of Peace and Justice*. Edited by Joseph Gremillion. Maryknoll: Orbis Books, 1976.

_____. 1979. "Final Document." *Puebla and Beyond*. Edited by John Eagleson and Philip Scharper. Maryknoll: Orbis Books.

Leo III. [1891]. "Rerum Novarum." *Catholic Social Thought: The Documentary Heritage*. Edited by David J. O'Brien and Thomas A. Shannon. Maryknoll: Orbis Books, 1992.

Lwaminda, Peter. "The African Background to the African Synod." *Catholic International*, Volume 2, No. 22 (December 15-31, 1991).

Meeking, Basil and John Stott, eds. 1986. *The Evangelical-Roman Catholic Dialogue on Mission: 1977-1984*. Exeter: The Paternoster Press.

O'Brien, David J. and Shannon, Thomas A. 1992. *Catholic Social Thought: The Documentary Heritage*. Maryknoll: Orbis Books.

_____. 1970. *Renewing the Earth: Catholic Documents on Peace, Justice and Liberation*. Garden City: Image Books.

Paul VI. [1975]. *Evangelii Nuntiandi*. Manila: Saint Paul Publications, 1985.

_____. [1967]. "Populorum Progressio". *The Gospel of Peace and Justice*. Edited by Joseph Gremillion. Maryknoll: Orbis Books, 1976.

Pius XI. [1931]. "Quadragesimo Anno." *Catholic Social Thought: The Documentary Heritage*. Edited by David J. O'Brien and Thomas A. Shannon. Maryknoll: Orbis Books, 1992.

Second Plenary Council. 1992. *Acts and Decrees of the Second Plenary Council of the Philippines*. Manila: Catholic Bishops Conference.

Synod of Bishops. [1971]. "Justice in the World." *The Gospel of Peace and Justice*. Edited by Joseph Gremillion. Maryknoll: Orbis Books, 1976.

Vatican Council II. [1965]. "Ad Gentes Divinitus." *Vatican Council II: The Conciliar and Post-Conciliar Documents*. Edited by Austin Flannery, O.P. Northport: Costello Publishing Company, 1975 and 1984.

_____. [1964]. "Lumen Gentium." *Vatican Council II: The Conciliar and Post-Conciliar Documents*. Edited by Austin Flannery, O.P. Northport: Costello Publishing Company, 1975 and 1984.

_____. "Unitatis Redintegratio." *Vatican Council II: The Conciliar and Post-Conciliar Documents*. Edited by Austin Flannery, O.P. Northport: Costello Publishing Company, 1975 and 1984.

Walsh, John J. 1983. "AMECA Seminar on the African Synod." *Catholic International*, Volume 3, No. 1 (January 1-14, 1992).

_____. *Evangelization and Justice*. Manila: Claretian Publications.

_____."Instruction on Certain Aspects of the Theology of Liberation." *Catholic Almanac* (1985).

_____."To Be Witnesses of Christ Who Has Set Us Free." *Catholic International*, Volume 3, No. 5 (March 1-14, 1992).

_____. "You Shall Be My Witnesses." *Catholic International*, Volume 2, No. 17 (October 1-14, 1991).